MW01198986

Day Trippin' Oklahoma

100

Unique Destinations

****

Knoel C. Honn

Dedication

This book is dedicated to my wife Wendy, grandsons, Charlie and Stanley, and to all of my extended family and friends in Oklahoma.

Contents

30. Ghost Town Picher, Oklahoma
31. Eagle Park Amusement Park
32. OKC Museum of Art
33. Gravity Hill
34. Mount Olive Cemetery
35. Woods of Southeastern Oklahoma
36. Oklahoma Capital Building
37. OKC Bombing Memorial
38. Factory Obscura
39. Pops Pop Bottle Sculpture
40. Toy and Action Figure Museum
41. Play Tower
42. OKC Underground
43. Tulsa Underground
44. Scottish Rite Temple
45. Boston Avenue United Methodist Church
46. DW Correll Museum
47. E.W. Marland Museum
48. Restored 1920's Gas Station
49. Atoka Museum and Civil War Cemetery
50. Woolaroc Museum and Wildlife Preserve
51. Life Size Metal Dinosaur
52. Tin Woodsman
53. Mickey Mantle Statue #1
54. Tom Mix Museum
55. World's Largest Peanut
56. VW Bug Spider Sculpture #1
57. The Castle of Muskogee
58. WWII Sub U.S.S. Batfish
59. Woody Guthrie Statue
60. Woody Guthrie Home Site and Tree
61. American Banjo Museum
62. Flaming Lips Alley
63. Mickey Mantle Statue #2
64. Vince Gill Statue
65. Pawnee Bill Museum
66. Frontier City Amusement Park
67. Giant Pioneer Woman and Museum
68. Standing Bear
69. Howdy Tire Man
70. Dinosaur and Space Rocket

Preface

Often Oklahoma gets a bad rap. In fact Oklahoma is a beautiful state full of all kinds of exciting adventures. Being a lifelong Okie, born and raised here, I have had my fair share of adventures. The culture in Oklahoma is rich and varied, from its Native American roots to it rock 'n roll roots. Like Tulsa, having birthed many rock legends, and the "Tulsa Sound," that enticed Eric Clapton and George Harrison. Oklahoma has an amazing art scene especially in Oklahoma City and Tulsa. The state was built on oil, but we must not forget the beauty of the plains, the lakes the rivers, the skylines, the historic venues, the many mansions that were a result of the oil boom, its haunted abandoned churches, amusement parks and abandoned buildings.

There is so much to do in Oklahoma you could drive all over the state and never run out of things to do. It was easy to come up with 100 things to go see. I could have easily done a list of 200. This list isn't ranked or in any particular order. I simply chose 100 places I have gone or found interesting that friends have gone to.

So let's support our beautiful state and small businesses. Let's keep our unique roadside attractions alive and in business. Let's keep exploring and finding more and more to do in our amazing state. I think I have something here for everyone. Enjoy!

Acknowledgments

Thanks to my friends and family for putting up with me and all of my many varied projects. I am a very busy Oklahoma music historian. I have also been working on a book about the underrated Oklahoma band THE CALL for a long time. Taking advantage of my down time on that project I got motivated to finish this project.

I sincerely enjoy writing and helping others find joy and interest in the things that I have discovered in my life. Thanks to all of my artist, musician, and crazy friends for constantly tell me about the new and exciting places they have discovered and gone to.

I hope you have many entertaining day trips like me.

****

Sites to See in Oklahoma

****

Church Studio – Tulsa, OK

The Church Studio, Located at 304 S. Trenton Tulsa, OK 74120. The church started in 1913 as Grace Methodist Episcopal Church. By 1929 it had become First United Brethren Church. By 1948 it had become the First Evangelical United Brethren Church and in 1961 it became the First Church of God. Originally a brick church the current stone facade was added in the mid 1950's. In the early 1970's it wound up in the hands of Leon Russell and Denny Cordell who opened the studio and owned the Shelter Records label. Leon recorded there as well as many other famous musicians such as The Dwight Twilley Band, The GAP Band, Tom Petty and JJ Cale. After Leon's era other artists such as Roy Clark, The Tractors, Hanson and more have recorded there. The Studio is currently being renovated and is due to open the summer of 2021 along with a new museum just to the south of it. After visiting Church Studio go across the street to the Freeway Café and order some fantastic food. I recommend the fried green tomatoes.

Starting with the Church Studio the entire area has come back to life. Now called Studio Row, aka Leon Russell Road, Grammy award winning drummer David Teegarden Sr. set up his new studio just down 3rd street. To the south of Church Studio is a great record store selling all the latest vinyl as well as other great shops and restaurants. Spend the day exploring the area and then venture downtown if you have the time to see other great sites.

****

Church Studio 304 S. Trenton, Tulsa, OK. Shown here November 13, 2016 at Sunset the day Tulsa Legend Leon Russell passed away.

Church Studio under stewardship of owner Teresa Knox is currently undergoing the final stages of renovations and restoration. Just to the south of Church Studio a museum dedicated to Leon Russell is also in the final stages of construction.

Church Studio and the new museum will be open for business, events and visits in late 2021, so, make sure you come to Tulsa and visit the former studio of the Master of Space and Time.

Newly commissioned Leon Russell mural at 3rd & Trenton.

This new very large mural is across from Church Studio!
Located on Trenton and 3rd St. / Leon Russell Road.

Center of the Universe
Tulsa, OK

The Center of the Universe can be found in downtown Tulsa just northwest of the Jazz Hall of Fame which is located in the old Union Depot building. Located at the railroad overpass near South Boston Ave and Archer. The exact location is a small circle of bricks on the bridge north of the Iron Rain Cloud and Jazz Hall. When crossing the bridge if you stand in the concrete circle in the middle of the circle of bricks and talk you will hear an echo or reverberation that sounds as though you are standing in the center of the universe and everything is bouncing back to you. The exact cause is unknown. It was discovered after renovations in the early 1990's and is thought to occur as a result of sound bouncing back off of circular walls and other structures nearby. Just a short 5 minute drive from the Church Studio and a walk across the parking lot from the Jazz Hall of Fame.

The Golden Driller Statue Tulsa, OK

The Golden Driller Statue is located at the Tulsa fairgrounds 4145 E 21st Tulsa, OK 74114. The Golden Driller was originally built as a temporary structure in 1953. Later it was rebuilt out of steel covered in concrete and plaster and installed in its current location in 1966. He is 75 feet tall and 43,500 pounds. His right hand rests on a retired oil well moved there from Seminole, Oklahoma. He has been refurbished and modified a few times through the years. In more recent years he has been dressed to wear different shirts and in 2020 he had his face painted to look like Elon Musk to try to attract Tesla here. Make sure and pay the Driller a visit and take a few pictures next to this enormous golden landmark.

This landmark, during the Covid-19 pandemic is wore a blue medical face mask. Previously the Golden Driller has worn many different articles of clothing. In past years KMOD 97.5 radio has put a t-shirt on the Golden Driller as well as different themes from the Tulsa State Fair and other events occurring at the Tulsa fairgrounds.

You really have to visit the Golden Driller and take a picture by his boot to truly appreciate the sheer size of this historic monument to Tulsa and its one time title as the oil capital of the world.

The 75 foot Golden Driller in Tulsa, OK, on November 3rd, 2020 shown wearing a face mask during the global Covid-19 pandemic.

★★★★★★★★★4★★★★★★★★★

The Blue Whale
Catoosa, OK

The Blue Whale was built by Hugh Davis in the early 1970's just off route 66 in Catoosa, Oklahoma. Hugh Davis, a zoologist built the 80 ft long sperm whale out of pipe and concrete. It was constructed on property he owned by a pond as an anniversary gift for his wife Zelta of 34 years. It fell into disrepair and was eventually restored. Now open to the public again. It is located at 2600 N. Oklahoma 66, Catoosa, OK. It is on the north side of town, on the southbound side of Route 66. If you visit during the holidays you might even find ole blue lit up with holiday lights.

*********5**********

Cain's Ballroom – Tulsa, OK

One page to go into the history of Cain's Ballroom and why you should visit this landmark is laughable. In fact there is a documentary in the works that will do a much better job. That being said, Cain's Ballroom got its start in 1924. Built by Tate Brady the ballroom has been a garage, a dance joint, dance academy and a music venue like no other. Home to Bob Wills and the Texas Playboys from 1935 to 1942. Cain's helped popularize western swing music, hosting weekly dances and a midnight radio show. Cain's has a maple spring loaded dance floor like no other. Reinvented to its current state of being in the 70's it has hosted band's like the Sex Pistols, U2, The Call, Leon Russell, Jack White, Hanson, St. Vincent, They Might Be Giants and many, many more. If you are really lucky they might show you the spot where Sid Vicious punch a hole in the wall. So buy tickets to a show and check out this historic Oklahoma music venue. She's still looking good for being almost 100 years old.

Cain's Ballroom located at 423 N Main St, Tulsa, OK, across the street from the new OKPOP museum (coming in 2022), next to the walk of fame stars. Just blocks from great restaurants, other small venues and the Old Lady on Brady the Tulsa Theater (Formerly Brady Theater). A day trip to remember, and see similar music themed sites such as the Jazz Hall, Woody Guthrie Center and Church Studio all within 5 minutes of this historic location.

The signs at the historic Cain's Ballroom.

Giant Indian Chief Statue
Big Cabin, OK

Located in Big Cabin in front of the Big Cabin Travel Plaza. The "Standing Brave" statue is 46 feet tall on a five foot base. Built by Wade Leslie in 2000-2001, and found just off of highway 69 it's hard to miss. Woodshed Truck Stop 31209 S Hwy 69, Big Cabin, OK 74332. Standing Brave is one of many Native American themed statues and sculptures in Northeastern Oklahoma.

Leon Russell Monument
Tulsa, OK

Born Claude Russell Bridges April 2nd 1942. Leon died November 13th, 2016. Steve Todoroff, friend, and associate of Russell's, organized multiple fundraiser events over a period of two years. He raised over $50,000 to build this amazing monument to an amazing musician, pianist, vocalists, lyricist and so much more. One of the originators of the Tulsa Sound, he played with Joe Cocker, George Harrison and Elton John to name a few. He influenced generations of Tulsa musicians. Leon was interred there November 2018, almost exactly two years after he passed. The monument is located in Memorial Park Cemetery not far from Bob Wills, Sam Kinison and Rev. Billy Joe Daugherty. On the Southeast corner of 51st and Memorial, Section 15E, Court 9, Estate 1, Space 4.

Whether he is "Tulsa's Mayor of Rock N Roll," or "The Master of Space and Time," Leon Russell lives on in the hearts and souls of Oklahomans everywhere. So, take a day trip back to Tulsa one more time, because "Home Sweet Oklahoma" is on your mind.

Stay awhile and have a chat with Leon. You might even run into a few Leon Lifers. Some of the nicest people you will ever meet.

The Leon Russell monument located in Memorial Park Cemetery at 51ˢᵗ & Memorial in Tulsa, OK.

The Praying Hands Sculpture Tulsa, OK

The "Praying Hands," originally called "The Healing Hands" sculpture was first located out front of the ORU City of Faith medical center towers. The hands are 60 ft tall and over 30 tons of pure bronze. Now located on the campus of ORU (Oral Roberts University) at 7777 S. Lewis Ave., Tulsa, OK. They were moved after the City of Faith closed. The sculpture is said to be the largest bronze sculpture in the world. Not to mention the other structures on the ORU campus and the CityPlex Towers across the street are quite the site to see as well.

Philbrook Museum and Gardens – Tulsa, OK

Located a couple of blocks east of Peoria in a neighborhood. The estate at 2727 S. Rockford Road Tulsa, OK, is an amazing 20's villa structure with equally impressive gardens out back. Then there is the absolutely incredible collection of art. The Philbrook was originally home to oil pioneer Waite Phillips. The museum opened in 1939 and houses an impressive permanent collection as well as hosts numerous temporary exhibits annually. Located not far from downtown Tulsa and the Brookside district just down Peoria you can make a day of Art, Food and shopping all within 1 mile and 5 minutes.

Check the hours and days the museum is open at their website philbrook.org

Woody Guthrie Center
Tulsa, OK

Located in downtown Tulsa just a few blocks from Cain's Ballroom, The Center of the Universe, Tulsa Theater, Magic City Books, Guitar House and numerous places to grab some great food. 102 E Reconciliation Way, Tulsa, OK. You'll know you've arrived by the large mural of Woody Guthrie on the West wall playing his iconic guitar inscribed with "This Machine Kills Fascists." The Woody Guthrie Center has a great permanent exhibit about Woody and his life. It also hosts numerous traveling exhibits and events. If you are a music fan and coming to see similar sites in Tulsa you won't want to miss this one.

Oklahoma Jazz Hall of Fame Tulsa, OK

Located at 5 S. Boston Ave Tulsa, OK the Oklahoma Jazz hall is just a short jump, skip and a hop away from several other historic sites in downtown Tulsa. In the old Union Depot building just north of the Williams Tower. You can park and enjoy the exhibits and periodic events it hosts. When you are done you can walk across the parking lot to the "Iron Rain Cloud" sculpture and a few more feet to experience the Center of the Universe. Making this quite a destination that offers something for three of your five senses. Want to satisfy your other two senses go grab some great food downtown just a few blocks away.

The Gilcrease Museum
Tulsa, OK

Just west of downtown Tulsa, located at 1400 N Gilcrease Museum Road, take the Gilcrease Museum Road exit off of highway 412 and head north. Gilcrease is home to the world's largest collection of art from the American West, as well as, hosts a collection of items from Central and South America. Founded by Thomas Gilcrease in 1943, he deeded the property and collection to the city of Tulsa in 1958. Don't miss this fine collection just a 10 minute drive from other local museums and restaurants. See more information at www.gilcrease.org

Large statue out front of Gilcrease Museum Tulsa, OK.

*********13*********

Davis Gun Museum
Claremore, OK

Located just off of historic Route 66 in Claremore, JM Davis Gun Museum (330 N. J M Davis Blvd, Claremore, OK) offers a lot to the gun and weapons enthusiast. The museum boasts over 20,000 firearms and gun related items, as well as, non-firearm items such as spurs, beer steins and saddles. The museum has family friendly multi-media exhibits. So, take a day trip to Claremore and see the world's largest privately held collection of firearms. This museum won't disappoint.

*********14*********

The Tulsa Zoo – Tulsa, OK

The Tulsa Zoo is located in Mohawk Park at 6421 E 36th St N, Tulsa. It is 85 acres and opened in 1927. In 2005 the Tulsa Zoo was named America's Favorite Zoo. The zoo consists of several various exhibits and habitats including: The Lost Kingdom complex with Malayan Tigers, Snow Leopards, Chinese Alligators, Siamangs, Binturongs and Komodo Dragons; Robert J. LaFortune Wild Life Trek; Lost Kingdom Elephants; The Rainforest; The Chimpanzee Connection and much, much more. Come early and stay all day at Tulsa Zoo.

The OKC Zoo – OKC, OK

The Oklahoma City Zoo, about 2 hours west of the Tulsa Zoo, is a zoo and botanical gardens on 119 acres and home to more than 1,900 animals. Open all year long except Thanksgiving, Christmas and New Years, it is located at 2000 Remington Pl, Oklahoma City. The zoo has many unique exhibits including the wonders of wildlife and wild places exhibit. World-class habitats including Great EscApe, Cat Forest/Lion Overlook and the Oklahoma Trails and Sanctuary Asia, where you will find the amazing animals of the Asian continent. So, plan a weekend in OKC for the zoo and it's many other exciting experiences.

Take the kids and stay all day!

(405)424-3344

**********16*********

The Omniplex / Planetarium OKC, OK

The Omniplex Science Museum and Kirkpatrick Planetarium. Located at 2100 NE 52nd St. Oklahoma City, Oklahoma. This science museum started in 1958 and moved to its permanent location in 1962. The Oklahoma Air and Space Museum was added in 1980. In 1985 the Kirkpatrick Gardens and Greenhouse was added, and then the OmniDome Theater, Oklahoma's first large-format, dome-screen theater, opened in 2000. Other features are the CurioCity Childrens Museum, Destination Space with a command module simulator, The International Photography and Hall of Fame and much more. Get more information at www.sciencemuseumok.org

Free use image: courtesy Nasa.gov

Buck Atoms – Tulsa, OK

Buck Atom's Cosmic Curios on historic route 66. On 11th street near Peoria. 1347 E 11th St, Tulsa. Opens 7 days a week most of the year. Home to the 21 ft tall Buck Atom Space Cowboy statue. This curious little shop has unique gifts and knick-knacks for everyone. t-Shirts, postcards, bumper stickers, unique original art and sculptures, snacks and so much more. So, come check out the most unique "Muffler Man" on the Mother Road and buy some gifts and treats from Mary Beth at Buck Atom's Cosmic Curios.

Buck Atom's on 11th Street near Peoria in Tulsa, OK

The amazing Buck Atom Sculpture based on the vintage roadside "Muffler Man" statues of yesteryear. Day Trip and check out this great curio shop / roadside attraction.

The Meadow Gold Sign Tulsa, OK

The Meadow Gold milk sign is a neon sign originally built in 1934. The building it first resided on was demolished in 2004. The sign was removed and restored coming back to life in 2009 on a dedicated structure on Route 66 near 11th and S. Peoria. 1 block from Buck Atom's Cosmic Curios and a very short drive to downtown Tulsa, Church Studio and Brookside. Centrally located to many exciting day trip destinations. So, go visit Buck Atom's, get a cold root beer in a bottle and walk down the street to take pictures under this amazing neon sign from yesteryears.

**********19**********

The Gathering Place
Tulsa, OK

A nationally recognized park, and outdoor space, which opened September 2018. Located at 2650 S John Williams Way, Tulsa. Featuring sports courts, an Adventure Playground, Sky Hill, Swing Garden, Skate Park and many more family friendly options. Built on a flat Stretch of land overlooking the Arkansas River, this unusual park offers something for everyone. Bring the kids, bring that special someone, or simply bring a book and enjoy this great outdoor destination. Like many Tulsa destinations the Gathering Place is locate just minutes from downtown.

Leon Russell's Murals Downtown – Tulsa, OK

With the resurgence of the Tulsa music scene many unique murals have popped up around town in conjunction with the monuments, museums and venues. Tulsa continues to tip its top hat to the Master of Space and Time Leon Russell. In the last couple of years since Leon's passing two amazing murals have popped up downtown.

Mural number one is located at 415 E 3rd St, Tulsa. Created by artist JEKS a black and white portrait of Leon Russell in his top hat, backlit by pink roses. "Such a sight to see," in this bustling downtown district near plenty of unique shops and food.

Mural number two is a unique colorful take on MOSAT wearing his sunglasses with his hair swooping in the wind. This mural of Leon Russell takes up an entire outside wall at Hale Factor near 4th Street and Norfolk Avenue. Local artist Josh Butts created the tribute in just three hours.

So come to Tulsa to see the many Leon Russell sites. Check out the two murals, the monument at Memorial park, Church Studio and even Cain's Ballroom where Leon Russell once played.

Rumor has it that there is another mural and still even more unique Leon Russell sites yet to come.

The above mural at 415 E 3rd St, Tulsa, OK

Bottom mural west wall of building at 4th and Norfolk Ave.

************21***********

Tulsa Fairground Flea Market – Tulsa, OK

The Tulsa (Fairgrounds) Flea Market opened back in 1972. Originally just a handful of vendors, it has now grown to host hundreds of vendors in various locations on the Tulsa Fairgrounds. Often, this flea market is found in the upper level of the Expo. This flea market is a Tulsa favorite featuring a wide array of unique, vintage, collectible and rare items. Vintage Vinyl LP's, Books, Military items, Toys, Jewelry and so much more. Spend hours looking and haggling on the many bargains to be found. Located between Harvard and Yale on 21st street. Check out dates and times online at tulsafleamarket.net. While you are there you can check out the Golden Driller out front of the Expo building.

Robbers Cave State Park
Wilburton, OK

Robbers Cave State Park located in Latimer county at 4575 Northwest 1024th Ave, Wilburton, was designated as such in 1936. Located near the scenic hilly woodlands of the Sans Bois Mountains of southeast Oklahoma. This scenic destination is a favorite of rappellers, equestrians, hikers and outdoor lovers. Named for the famous outlaw cave hidden in the sandstone hills and cliffs. There is 3,800 acres of hunting grounds and fishing. 26 cabins are available. There are 250 acres of ATV tracks with some seasonal accommodations including certain campsites, swimming pools and restrooms. Mini golf, paddle boat rentals and golf carts are also available.

Check availability online at:
https://www.travelok.com/state-parks/robbers-cave-state-park

Grand Lake – Northeast, OK

Grand Lake or Grand Lake o' the Cherokees is located in northeastern Oklahoma, in the foothills of the Ozark Mountain Range. It is offers a wide range of entertainment and activities. Located in Delaware / Ottawa / Mayes / and Craig counties and the cities of Grove and Disney.

If you are looking to go fishing you are sure to find Channel catfish, White crappie, Smallmouth bass, Largemouth bass & Bluegill. Enjoy a day out on the boat, water skiing and getting some sun. The surface area of the lake covers 46,500 acres. You can find everything from luxury living to rustic cabins. There is a wide variety of restaurants and bars at Grand Lake. Take time to check out Monkey Island and find the many great locations it has to offer.

Check out https://grandlakeliving.com/ and plan your day trip or extended stay today!

Blue Hole Park – Salina, OK

Blue Hole Park is a seasonal park centered around a deep blue natural spring fed swimming hole, with tent and RV camping, and on-site concessions. Located at 158 N 4470, Salina, OK, you won't be disappointed with this relaxing family friendly destination. There are also a limited number of cabins and one RV available to rent. Surrounded by woods and wildlife you will be hard pressed to find a comparable destination in the state of Oklahoma.

*********25*********

Optimus Prime Transformer Robot – Stillwater, OK

Optimus Prime is located at one of the two G&M Body Shop's in Stillwater, OK. This transformer is one of two Transformer statues in Stillwater and one of only five in the United States that are 20 ft or taller! The Optimus Prime Transformer is located on the south side of Highway 51 on the east side of Stillwater just past S. Jardot Rd. The exact address is 2207 E. 6th Ave. Stillwater, OK. So, take a day trip to Stillwater explore the historic OSU campus, eat at Joe's and go check out Optimus Prime and the other local Transformer Bumblebee.

Stars Walk of Fame (by Cains Ballroom) – Tulsa, OK

One of the lesser know attractions in downtown Tulsa is the Stars Walk of Fame on the sidewalk out front of Cain's Ballroom. 423 N Main Street. There is an array of Okies and adopted Okies forever emblazoned out front of the Tulsa landmark venue. The walk of fame came about in 2003 with the refurbishing of the ballroom. With OKPOP museum going in across the street, in time more famous Okies may join the elite few already remembered there. So, if you are visiting Cain's, OKPOP or just enjoying a casual day downtown go check out the stars of Leon Russell, JJ Cale, Roy Clark and other notable Okies, and take a picture with the star of your musical hero.

OKPOP Museum – Tulsa, OK

OKPOP museum is an exciting new destination being built across from Cain's Ballroom at 422 N Main St, Tulsa. Expected to open in 2022, it is a new 25 million dollar pop culture museum. The inspiration for the museum came from a book put out in 2009 called Another Hot Oklahoma Night based on a song from THE CALL, an 80's rock band. THE CALL was founded by fellow Okies Michael Been and Scott Musick. The Museum will have all types of pop culture exhibits and feature musicians such as Leon Russell, JJ Cale, THE CALL and more.

www.okpop.org

Rendering of museum to open in 2022.

World's Largest Totem Pole
Foyil, OK

Bricktown District – OKC, OK

Bricktown is a revitalized warehouse district in Oklahoma City that is now home to great food and entertainment. Bricktown showcases a wide array of restaurants, bars, eclectic retail shops and even a water taxi that gives rides up and down the canal that is down the middle of the district. The canal taxi offers tours and dinner cruises for a unique experience not found anywhere else in Oklahoma. In the summer take a leisure stroll in the cool breeze along the canal. In the winter enjoy the holiday lights and the seasonal goods that the shops have to offer. Make sure and check out this ever evolving destination. You can't go wrong spending your day in Bricktown.

So come on down to Bricktown.

Abandoned Ghost Town Picher, OK

I'm sure you've heard the "abandoned ghost town" pitch a million and one times. Except when it comes to Picher, Oklahoma; it seems to have the goods. Picher was once a mining town providing large quantities of lead and zinc to the U.S. especially during WWII. The town is now contaminated with tailings from its mining days. The buildings are dangerously undermined and a tornado several years back destroyed many of the local houses speeding up the exodus of the dying town. Rumor has it that the last few remaining residents vacated in 2015. Much of the original buildings have been destroyed. The remainder of this old mining town sits empty and decaying waiting for the government to eventually clean up the town and its haunted poison past. Remnants of the town can be still be seen driving down the main roads that are still open to the public. So, bring your camera and check out the last few ghost town sites.

Eagle Park Amusement Park Cache, OK

This now deserted amusement park was built in 1957 and abandoned in 1985. Originally a farm / ranch the owner decided to start adding old salvaged buildings and amusement park rides. The park was open each year from Easter to Labor Day. The park offered horse rides for a $1.00 an hour. The horses could be rode anywhere on the property. It eventually had about 20 small buildings creating a small town. The park also had a skating rink that one could skate all day for a mere $1.50.

The park now stands vacant and abandoned. Be sure you don't trespass without permission as there is still a resident landowner on the property that doesn't take kindly to trespassers. To get permission to go on the property to take pictures go to the Trading Post or call (580) 429-3420 for an appointment.

Many of the rides and structures are still present on the property. The future hope and goal is to raise money to restore the property to be a safe walk around park primarily to be used as location to take pictures or to have outdoor events.

Don't miss out on this creepy yet entertaining destination.

OKC Museum of Art
OKC, OK

Located at 415 Couch Drive, Oklahoma City, OK, 73102 in the heart of downtown OKC. Call (405) 236-3100 for hours of operation and more information.

This museum offers a wide range of traveling and permanent exhibits from around the world. The museum's permanent collection boasts one of the world's largest public collections of Dale Chihuly glass, the photography of Brett Weston, and the definitive collection of work by the Washington color painter Paul Reed.

Mere minutes from many other exciting locations in central Oklahoma City, this is a day trip destination that is hard to pass up.

Gravity Hill – Bartlesville, OK

Sure to trip you out and give you a few moments pause… Gravity Hill in Bartlesville Oklahoma makes you go "Huh?" This unusual day trip location is worth the drive. How many places do you know of in Oklahoma where you can park your car seemingly facing downhill and disengage the brake and see your car roll backwards up the hill? Also known as Magnetic Hill the phenomenon though not unique to Oklahoma is one you will sure want to experience when you are near Bartlesville checking out other sites such as the Price Tower designed by Frank Lloyd Wright.

The hill is an optical illusion that will catch you off guard. Make sure and plan this as one of your destinations for your day trip to Bartlesville, Oklahoma.

Mount Olive Cemetery Hugo, OK

If you are into local history, genealogy, music or even the circus this cemetery will offer a lot of intrigue. Oklahoma music legend Phil Seymour (Solo artist and founding member of The Dwight Twilley Band) is laid to rest here.

The final resting place for many rodeo greats including: Freckles Brown, Lane Frost, Todd Watley, and L. Hammock. Ed Ansley, better known as Buster Brown, and William H. Darrough, the founder of Hugo, are also buried here. Hugo was a winter home for many circuses; a special area is set aside called Showmen's Rest, which features unusual headstones and gravesites for circus performers and owners. Guided tours can be arranged for groups upon request.

Mount Olive Cemetery is located at Trice & S 8th St, Hugo, OK, 74743. For more information contact them at : hugo-chamber@sbcglobal.net

Hugo is about 3 hours south of Tulsa (9 miles north of the Oklahoma - Texas state line) and also offers other interesting day trip destinations such as The Frisco Depot Museum, the Endangered Ark Foundation, and the Choctaw County Genealogical Society Research Library. So, go check out what this little Oklahoma town has to offer today.

Woods of Southeastern OK
Honobia, OK

This day trip destination offers a variety of reasons to go explore. Everything from hunting and fishing, to the annual Bigfoot Festival. You should go check out the beauty of nature in southeastern Oklahoma. Honobia Creek WMA covers 91,721.18 acres in Pushmataha, Leflore, and McCurtain counties. Honobia Creek WMA is a mix of pine and hardwood forests. Nonresidents are required to purchase an $85 annual permit, no exemptions. There are many game species such as: deer, bears, quail, turkey, rabbit, squirrel, dove, waterfowl, coyote, bobcat, grey fox, beaver and raccoons. No designated camping areas available, but primitive camping is allowed everywhere on the WMA. Lodging and restaurants are available in Clayton.

For more information check with:
Hugo Area Chamber of Commerce
200 South Broadway
Hugo OK 74743
(580) 326-7511
hugochamber@lstarnet.com
http://www.hugochamber.com

or the:
Kiamichi Country Tourism Office
1-800-722-8180

Oklahoma Capital Building
OKC, OK

Taking you back to school for a brief history lesson is our Oklahoma State Capital Building. Oklahoma became a state in 1907. The Capital Building began construction in 1914 and was completed in 1917. It originally was home to the Oklahoma state judicial branch. The judicial branch moved to a new home in 2011. The Oklahoma Supreme Court hearing chambers remains at the Capital Building.

The structure itself is very ornate. It is a reinforced concrete structure covered with granite and limestone. The building has an ornate dome and stone lions on the corners of the copper roof. Though originally it did not have a dome it was built in a manner to support one. In 2001 construction of a dome began thanks to funding of a 21 million dollar state fund for the project. Completed in November 2002 the dome is now adorned with a twenty-two-foot-tall bronze statue called "The Guardian," created by artist and state senator Enoch Kelly Haney of Seminole.

In the bustling heart of Oklahoma City, our amazing state capital is located near many other amazing day trip attractions, such as, the next two day trip destinations.

The Oklahoma capital building is located at:
22nd St. and Lincoln Boulevard, OKC, OK.

OKC Bombing Memorial
OKC, OK

On April 19, 1995, outside the Alfred P. Murrah Federal Building in Oklahoma City, Oklahoma, the Oklahoma City bombing occurred. A truck packed with explosives was detonated killing 168 people. The blast, set off by anti-government militant Timothy McVeigh, also left hundreds more injured. A sad chapter in Oklahoma history that forever changed the landscape of OKC, and brought about the creation of this heartfelt memorial to those we lost that day.

The deceased sadly included 19 young children who were in the building's day care center at the time of the blast. More than 650 other people were injured in the bombing. The explosion also damaged or destroyed over 300 other buildings in the immediate area.

May 1995, the Murrah Federal Building was demolished and the Oklahoma City National Memorial Museum later opened at the site.

The memorial features the Gates of Time, a reflecting pool, field of empty chairs, survivors wall, memorial fence, the Alfred P. Murrah Federal Building Plaza and much more. Located at 620 N Harvey Ave, Oklahoma City, OK, 73102. Tickets currently range from $12 - $15 each.

Factory Obscura – OKC, OK

Is one of many locations in OKC related to, and inspired by, the incredibly creative and ever evolving rock band The Flaming Lips. A unique band coming out of the 1990's OKC band scene, that continues cranking out original music to this day. The exterior of the building was painted by the band and the current owners expanded on the concept and trippy vibe.

Factory Obscura coming from that creative vibe states on thier website, "The future is collaborative."

"FACTORY OBSCURA IS AN OKLAHOMA CITY-BASED ART COLLECTIVE CREATING IMMERSIVE EXPERIENCES THAT AWAKEN WONDER, BUILD COMMUNITY, AND MAKE THE WORLD BETTER."

Check out www.factoryobscura.com for the latest information on events and installations. Worth the day trip to OKC! Check it out you won't be disappointed.

Located at 25 NW 9th St, Oklahoma City, OK 73102

Email: info@factoryobscura.com

If you love the artistic creative vibe then this place is must to check out and then go back again and do something completely different each time.

Pops Pop Bottle Sculpture Arcadia, OK

Reportedly the World's largest pop bottle and soda store. In 2007 a 66-foot-tall soda bottle sculpture was erected dubbed "Bubbles," and an accompanying soda-centered location named "Pops," debuted on Route 66, the vision of billionaire Aubrey K. McClendon, who owned much of the surrounding land.

The soda bottle is made out of stacked steel hoops lit up with thousands of color-shifting lights. "Pops" is known for its selection of 700+ varieties of soda and other bottled refreshments.

The windows of "Pops" are lined with shelves of bottled soda, and sunlight streams through the soda bottles creating an effect similar to stained-glass windows.

So, if you find yourself in this neck of the woods or simply love soda and want a fizzy day trip to paradise. Drive the station wagon, so, you can bring back several cases of your favorite fizzy bottles of joy from "Pops."

Don't forget to take a few pictures of the giant soda bottle that is so large even the Golden Driller couldn't chug it... Just maybe the Praying Hands could manage it on a hot summer day.

Toy & Action Figure Museum – Pauls Valley, OK

Located at 111 S Chickasaw St, Pauls Valley, OK, 73075 the Toy and Action Figure Museum in Pauls Valley, Oklahoma is a wonder to behold. Currently boasting over 13,000 Action Figures and Toys it is currently only $7 to get in and see Kevin Stark's unique collection.

Kevin started out with a mere 11,000 toys and action figures. He bought a warehouse and opened the museum in 2005. The collection has gradually grown to what it is today. The museum also has a play room for kids and adults that never outgrew it.

Call 405-238-6300 for days and times the museum is open.

Play Tower – Bartlesville, OK

Continuing with a theme of young hearted fun, take a day trip to the Play Tower in Bartlesville. After boring the kids with your trip to check out the Frank Lloyd Wright designed Price Tower take a quick jaunt to the kid friendly Play Tower. Located in Sooner Park at 231 SE Quail Ridge Loop, Bartlesville, OK 74006. The Play Tower was designed by midcentury architect Bruce Goff, commissioned by Mrs. H.C. Price wife of founder of the H.C. Price Company in 1963. A restoration campaign in 2013 was focused on restoring the retro-future tower for its 50th anniversary. The restored tower was unveiled the following year.

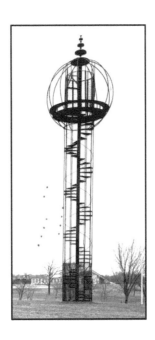

OKC Underground – OKC, OK

The downtown Oklahoma City Underground (formerly known as the Concourse) is an array of tunnels and skywalks that connect many of the downtown buildings in OKC. Opened in 1974, the tunnels are about one mile long and covers more than 20 square blocks.

The OKC Underground is open to the public from 6 a.m. to 8 p.m., Monday through Friday. There are many businesses located in the underground including a cafe, a Chinese restaurant, a post office, and a bank. The underground hosts many photo galleries and art installations.

For more information about exploring the tunnels and checking out the many underground offerings call: (405) 235-3500. Email: info@downtownokc.com or
go online to: https://downtownokc.com/underground/

If you want to spend some time exploring OKC or you are lucky enough to live nearby you'll want to spend a few days at the museum, in the underground, in its many book and record stores and maybe even at the OKC Zoo; with or without the kiddos.

Tulsa Underground
Tulsa, OK

And if one underground wasn't enough… Try going to Tulsa next to see what its downtown underground has to offer you.

Beneath downtown Tulsa, a system of secret underground tunnels lurk. The tunnels were built to connect many of Tulsa's skyscrapers. The tunnel system was originally designed for freight, but soon became a highway protecting the wealthy and elite from danger.

You can take a self guided tour in about 30 minutes to an hour depending on how many pictures you take. For more information and an online map go check out the website at https://www.tulsa.tours/tulsa-tunnel-tour and get ready for an intriguing experience.

You'll probably want to start at the Hyatt Hotel and take the 3rd street tunnel to the 320 S. Boston Building. Next you will go from 320 S. Boston to the Kennedy Building to Mid-Continent Building. You'll eventually go through the Atlas Life Building, The Philtower and the Philcade.

Don't miss out on a great cup of coffee at the end of your journey in the Topeka Philcade.

Scottish Rite Temple
Guthrie, OK

Touted as one of the world's largest Masonic centers, the great Temple of the Scottish Rite of Freemasonry in Guthrie is a place where (according to their website) the, "glory of the Grand Architect of the Universe is celebrated and the aim of human progress is affirmed–a place of study and education, recreation and fellowship, learning and reflection, charity and compassion. A place where one can expect the human spirit to be lifted and the brotherhood of man embraced."

Why take a day trip to this location? Located at 900 E Oklahoma Ave, Guthrie, OK, 73044 this grand looking temple was built at the height of the oil boom in an "ostentatious style."

Opening in 1919 this 101 year old temple and philosophy is welcoming to visitors year round. For more information call: (405) 282-1281. Whether for the architecture or "enlightenment" you're sure to find this an intriguing day trip destination.

The next time you are heading in the direction of Guthrie, OK, or just have free day to satisfy your curiosity stop by the Scottish Rite Temple and check it out.

Boston Ave. United Methodist Church – Tulsa

When you are done with Tulsa's Underground, #43 on the list, meander on south to the Boston Avenue United Methodist Church. Much like a lot of Tulsa's architecture this church will not disappoint. Located at 1301 S Boston Ave, Tulsa, OK, 74119; the Boston Avenue United Methodist Church was completed in 1929. The church is considered to be one of the finest examples of ecclesiastical Art Deco architecture in the United States. Boston Avenue has been placed on the National Register of Historic Places.

The congregation is over 125 years old. The building is over 90 years old. The location has undergone many renovations and additions but still retains the original Art Deco design and original aesthetic. In 2000 a columbarium sacred space where church members' cremains could be inurned at death was added. Much like the little cemeteries adjacent to country churches, where family members can come and remember those they love, the columbarium has indeed become a sacred space.

The exterior architecture is used by many as an ornate backdrop for a variety of pictures. If you are interested in Deco architecture or religious structures. Make Boston Avenue one of your many stops in downtown Tulsa when you visit.

DW Correll Museum
Catoosa, OK

This museum consists of two buildings. The main building has a mural painted on the exterior by award winning artist Lance Hunter. He was commissioned to pay tribute to D.W. Correll. The mural is 8 ft tall and 72 feet wide. The mural shows a peek into what you should expect in the museum. 19934 E Pine St., Catoosa, OK, 74015

Inside the main building, you will see a collection of rocks, gems, fossils and minerals from around the world. Also, as part of the collection, a unique assortment of sea shells and coral, jewelry, and a large collection of bottles and decanters.

In building number two is the car collection. The automobiles were restored by Mr. Correll, as well as, items such as the Texaco gas pump. Also on display is the 1904 Concert Stage horse-drawn carriage, alongside a collection of antique toy tractors, cars and pickups donated by Dan Ward. Antique automobiles include: 1898 Locomobile (Steam Engine), 1902 Oldsmobile Run About, 1906 Cadillac, 1914 Dodge Touring Car, 1914 Oldsmobile, 1917 Twin 6 Packard, 1919 Franklin, 1927 Stutz 8, 1930 Model A Ford Convertible, 1935 Ford 4-Door, 1948 Dodge Coupe. The D.W. Correll Museum has something for everyone. Take a day trip and check it out. For more information call 918-266-3612.

E.W. Marland Mansion
Ponca City, OK

The mansion is a 43,561 square ft. Mediterranean Revival-style mansion located at 901 Monument Rd, Ponca City, OK, 74604. Opened in 1928 and designated a historic landmark in 1977. The Mansion was designed and constructed as a showplace for fine art. When you tour the mansion you will learn the Marland story and about how the oil industry made it all possible.

1920's Restored Gas Station
Altus, OK

A vintage Phillips 66 gas station, located at: 210 S. Hudson St., Altus, OK. With vintage gas pumps out front, this little blast from the past is a roadside must see. Load up in your T-Bucket or your '58 Corvette and take a day trip to this great destination, and take some pictures of your car parked at this location frozen in time. While you are there go down the street to Missile Park and check out a vintage ICBM missile on display.

Atoka Museum & Civil War Cemetery – Atoka, OK

Do you have an interest in Civil War history, Oklahoma history, or just a history buff in general? You won't want to miss this great museum. Well worth the day trip to Atoka you can check out the cemetery and possibly do some genealogy research if your family is from this neck of the woods.

Located at 250 US-69, Atoka, OK, 74525 you can check out this great locations history and cultural exhibits, as well as, it's complete dinosaur skeleton. For more information call (580) 889-7192.

This property is managed by the Atoka Historical Society and is listed on the National Register of Historic Places. Sadly during the civil war a measles outbreak ravaged Confederate troops and the cemetery was created to bury the dead soldiers using crude sandstone head markers with their names and date of death etched in them.

Continued research at the National Archives confirmed the measles outbreak of 1862 and confirmed the identities of many of the soldiers.

Though the Civil War was a troubling time it is one that should not be forgotten. Plan your Oklahoma day trip now.

Woolaroc Museum & Wildlife Preserve

Woolaroc is located in Bartlesville, OK, at 1925 Woolaroc Ranch Rd. Woolaroc, a museum and wildlife preserve located in the Osage Hills of northeastern Oklahoma, on State Highway 123 roughly 12 mi SW of Bartlesville, and 45 miles north of Tulsa. Woolaroc, established in 1925, was the ranch retreat of oilman Frank Phillips.

Frank Phillips, the founder of Phillips Petroleum Company, created the Woolaroc preserve. The 3,700 acre wildlife preserve is home to more than thirty varieties of animals and birds. The location is a working ranch that maintains the animals for the enjoyment of guests in a natural and protected setting.

The museum houses one of the best western art collections in the world. You can also experience Frank Phillips' private collection of curiosities which includes a race-winning monoplane and the world's largest collection of Colt rifles.

So, if you liked the Davis Gun Museum in Claremore and are a big fan of wildlife and colt firearms this is the place for you. Plan your day trip now and go visit Woolaroc Museum and Wildlife Preserve today.

**********51**********

Life Size Metal Dinosaur Boise City, OK

This really cool Dinosaur sculpture is a site worth taking the kids to see. Whether you are a 5 year old, or a 50 year old kid at heart, go check out this amazing roadside attraction in Boise City. Located at 1300 N Cimarron Boise City, OK, 73933.

"Cimmy" the Dinosaur sits outside the Cimarron Heritage Center Museum. This metal Apatosaurus sculpture, measures 65 feet long, 35 feet high and weighs thousands of pounds, standing tall greeting visitors to the museum every day.

**********52**********

Tin Woodsman Sculpture Boise City, OK

Another exciting roadside attraction for the entire family. Also, located at 1300 N Cimarron St, Boise City, OK, at the Cimarron Heritage Center Museum. Go check out this great 13 ft. tall sculpture by John D. Morris today! Call for more information 580-544-3479.

Mickey Mantle Statue #1
Commerce, OK

Continuing with a reoccurring theme of sculptures and statues, we suggest paying a visit to Mickey Mantles statue in Commerce, OK. One of two Mickey Mantle statues in the state of Oklahoma this is something sure to be loved by the sports fans in your family. Mickey Mantle is one of the all time baseball greats. This statue located at 420 D St., Commerce, OK, stands beyond the center field fence of the Commerce High School baseball field. The statue and granite base stand over 9 ft tall and was dedicated in 2010. Mickey Mantle played for the Commerce High School baseball team after his family moved there when he was four years old. Mantle died in 1995 and is remembered as one of the all time greats of the sport.

Tom Mix Museum
Dewey, OK

Located at 721 N Delaware St, Dewey, OK, 74029, the museum contains a large selection of Tom Mixs' personal collection. A very colorful character on the silver screen and even one time Marshall of Dewey, Oklahoma. Tom Mix kept us entertained in the movies from 1909 to 1935.

Mix made 336 total feature films. He produced 88, wrote 71, and directed 117. He also made nine sound feature films and a fifteen-chapter serial called Miracle Rider. He was known for quick action and daredevil stunts. Tom and his horse were known for performing their own stunts.

So, take a day trip to Dewey and check out the other exciting adventures it has to offer as well. For more information call 918-534-1555.

*********55*********

World's Largest Peanut Durant, OK

Are you nuts for nuts? Then you'd want to come check out a peanut that is sure make even Mr. Peanut jealous. The world's largest peanut in Durant, OK. Well not really. In fact this peanut is not the world's largest but it claims to be. Out front of city hall, the monument has sat since 1974. Made of molded aluminum, the monument honors the peanut industry of surrounding Bryan county.

So, if you are a peanut nut, and taking a day trip to this neck of the woods, then you'll want to check it out and judge for yourself... Or maybe I'm just nuts??

**********56*********

VW Bug Spider Sculpture Lexington, OK

Just off of highway 77 near Lexington, Oklahoma, you will spot a "Strange Thing" for sure. Lexington's Black Widow inspired VW Bug spider sculpture. Okay sure this one only has six legs but it's still really cool to see. One of a growing array of similar bugs across the country this one is next to an old VW graveyard. So, if this is near your other Oklahoma day trip destinations go check it out!

**********57*********

The Castle of Muskogee Muskogee, OK

The Castle of Muskogee is located at 3400 W Fern Mountain Rd, Muskogee, OK, 74401. The Castle is host to many events throughout the year. Fireworks in June and July, an annual Renaissance Fair in May, and many other events and festivals. Check out their website at www.okcastle.com or call (918) 687-3625

This unique location has won many awards and continues to host unique experiences that everyone will love.

WWII Sub U.S.S. Batfish Muskogee, OK

Whether you are already in Muskogee, or visiting the Oklahoma Hall of Fame, or The Castle, you'll want to swing by and check out the U.S.S. Batfish WWII Submarine. Unique and educational for the kiddos or adults. Located at 3500 Batfish Rd, Muskogee, OK, 74403, the park it is located in also hosts memorials to fallen U.S. Soldiers. It is an impressive site to see. Make this part of your Muskogee day trip and check it out.

*********59*********

Woody Guthrie Statue Okemah, OK

Are you, like me, really into music and local music history? Then this is a must see stop on your Oklahoma day trip schedule. This statue of Woody Guthrie, also near Woody Guthrie murals, is located at 399-301 W Broadway St, Okemah, OK, 74859. Your trip to Okemah will be totally worthwhile as it is also home to the Woody Guthrie home site next on our list of fantastic day trips.

Woody Guthrie Home Site & Tree – Okemah, OK

Woody Guthrie. You could make a few days worth of Day Trippin' just dedicated to this folk singer with an opinion or two. From the Woody Guthrie Center in Tulsa, to the Statue and murals in Okemah, or the Home Site and Tree in Okemah. Woody Guthrie had a major impact on our state and is deservedly remembered. Located at N 1st Street & Birch Street in Okemah, OK, his boyhood home still stands along with a carved tree in memory of Woody. The high school he attended is also located at 704 E Date Street. Woody also has a street that was renamed after him in 1998. The street runs north and south from I-40 to Columbia Street in Okemah.

An additional stop is the Crystal Theater, a location where Woody Guthrie played early on. Located at 401 W Broadway Street, Okemah. A historic Woody Guthrie location that you want to make sure and visit. The theater is used for events and films including the annual Woody Guthrie Folk Festival.

Located at 411 W Broadway Street is the Okfuskee County History Center with many Woody Guthrie artifacts on exhibit. Finally before leaving town go by and visit the Woody Guthrie Memorial marker at Highland Cemetery just north of town on Woody Guthrie Blvd.

American Banjo Museum
OKC, OK

It is exactly what you would think it is... A museum dedicated to the history of the banjo. Located at 9 E. Sheridan Ave., Oklahoma City, OK, 73104. To get hours and days the museum is open you can call (405) 604-2793 or check it out online at americanbanjomuseum.com

This unique museum exhibits and documents the rise of the banjo. Starting with its arrival in North America up to modern times. The American Banjo Museum is home to the largest collection of banjos on public display in the world. Even if banjo isn't your thing this collection is sure to impress.

The museum was founded in 1998 in Guthrie and moved to Oklahoma City in 2009. The museum as of 2018 had over 400 banjos in its collection and had over 300 on display in its 21,000 sq ft facility.

The museums large collection also includes rare recordings, film, video, printed music and banjo ephemera and memorabilia. Whether you like country, folk or rock n roll music... guitar, uke or banjo this historic collection is sure to impress and be worth your time and $8 to get in.

Be prepared to spend some time looking at all of the vintage and historic banjos.

Flaming Lips Alley
OKC, OK

Obviously if you like my choices of destinations you are probably a music fan. Tulsa and Oklahoma City both have a lot to offer stemming from all of the impressive bands that Oklahoma has given birth to through the years.

The Flaming Lips has to be one of the most unique bands that have ever come out of Oklahoma. Frontman Wayne Coyne's unique outlook on life has spawned many unusual albums, events and even locations. Flaming Lips Alley in OKC is a Lips destination many a fan makes the journey to.

Located in the Bricktown district there is plenty to do and you never know who you might run into there. You might even bump into Wayne out on the town.

Mickey Mantle Statue #2
OKC, OK

The second statue of Mickey Mantle is similar to the first statue in Commerce but this one is of Mantle batting left handed. Being a switch hitter Mantle is batting right handed in Commerce. This bronze Mickey Mantle stands outside the third base entrance to RedHawks Field at Bricktown. The statue is over 8 ft tall and weighs over a ton. Mantle was born and raised in Oklahoma. He is depicted as if he just slugged one of his famous home runs. He is a Hall of Famer and played for the New York Yankees.

Vince Gill Statue – OKC, OK

Located at 2820 N May Ave, Oklahoma City, OK, 73107. On the east side of May Ave., north of NW 27th St., in front of the Classen High School auditorium. The 9 ½ foot tall statue was built to honor Vince and unveiled in 2014. So, if you are in OKC "Day Trippin'" make sure and swing by this impressive tribute to Vince.

Pawnee Bill Museum
Pawnee, OK

The home of Wild West show entertainer, Gordon W. "Pawnee Bill" Lillie. Located in Pawnee, Oklahoma and known as the Blue Hawk Peak Ranch or the Pawnee Bill Ranch and Museum. Covering about 500 acres and located at 1141 Pawnee Bill Rd, Pawnee, OK, 74058. The ranch consists of a historic home, modern museum and is a bison preserve with a herd of bison, longhorn cattle and horses on it.

The house was built in 1910. After the house was built many other buildings were added. A carriage house, log cabin, blacksmith shop, and observation tower were eventually added. In 1926 a three story barn was built.

In 1975 the site was added to the National Register of Historic Places. Since 1962 the site has been owned by the State of Oklahoma. The site is now operated by the Oklahoma Historical Society. The ranch is not only educational but hosts a yearly reenactment of Pawnee Bills Wild West Show.

For more information call (918) 762-2513. If you like a little bit of the old west vibe make sure and plan a day trip to check out the Pawnee Bill Ranch and museum.

Frontier City Amusement Park – OKC, OK

Like our family, many of you have kids and grandkids that enjoy taking family friendly day trips. Frontier City won't disappoint if you love a classic amusement park. Located in Oklahoma City just off of Hwy 35 at 11501 North I- 35 Service Rd, Oklahoma City, OK, 73131. Built in 1958 on 55 acres, Frontier City, a western theme park, is operated by Six Flags. For more information on park hours call (405) 478-2140. In recent years the park has undergone many renovations and ride updates. The park also hosts numerous summer concerts every year at the Starlight Amphitheater. The concerts are included with the park admission. So, make sure and check it out with the family.

Giant Pioneer Woman & Museum – Ponca City, OK

The Giant Pioneer Woman and Son was unveiled in 1930. The statue is an impressive 17-foot-tall monument of an Oklahoma mom, holding the hand of her son and was once the 3rd largest bronze statue in the world. The adjoining museum showcases a collection of pioneer artifacts. Located at 701 Monument Rd, Ponca City, OK, is a site worth seeing. The statue is free and the museum is only $7. Tuesday - Saturday 10m – 5pm.

*********68*********

Standing Bear – Ponca City

Located at 601 Standing Bear Parkway, Ponca City, OK, 74601. The Standing Bear Park, Museum and Education Center in Ponca City is a tribute to Native Americans with a 22-foot bronze statue of Ponca Chief Standing Bear. This monument sits on a 63-acre park. This day trip destination tells the history of American Indians in Oklahoma. Make sure you take the time to experience the peaceful memorial grove and the beauty of the pond and outdoor interpretive center.

Howdy Tire Man
Roosevelt, OK

This unusual artistic sculpture of a man made of tires stands 15 feet tall and waves a "Howdy" sign at passers by. There are two others around town. This one is located right beside the high school on highway 183 (if you are heading north it will be on west side of the road). So, if you are out that way make a stop in Roosevelt to check out its growing population of tire men.

Dinosaur & Space Rocket
Rush Springs, OK

As an artist and Oklahoma day tripper I really enjoy destinations like this one. A local farmer in Rush Springs, OK, has taken to turning old farm equipment into roadside sculptures like this dinosaur and rocket ship.

Located on US 81 between Chickasha, Oklahoma, and the Texas state line on the west hand side of the road. It's easy to see from the road. Go check it out.

Sequoyah's Cabin
Sallisaw, OK

Located at 470288 OK-101, Sallisaw, OK, 74955. Built in 1829 by Sequoyah, it served as his home from 1829 to 1844. Sequoyah created a written language for the Cherokee Nation in 1821. The historic log cabin and historic site off stands just off of Oklahoma State Highway 101 near Akins, Oklahoma. For information about operating hours call (918) 775-2413.

The cabin was enclosed in a protective stone building in 1936. The museum exhibits explains Cherokee history and basics of Sequoyah's written language. There are many exhibits and artifacts of early Cherokee life and items that reflect the accomplishments of Sequoyah and his contribution to early Oklahoma heritage located on a ten acre park. Visitors will enjoy a day trip walking the very grounds Sequoyah once walked.

The price of admission currently is $5 or less and worth the time to day trip to this great location for a bit of local culture and Oklahoma history.

If you are a member of the Cherokee Nation or are a member of any Native American tribe you should really come check out this day trip destination.

Burial Ground in Parking Lot
Sand Springs, OK

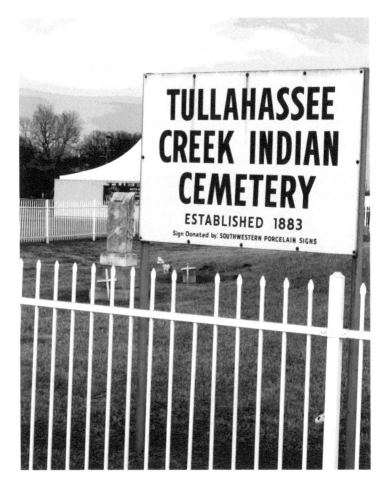

Just south of Hwy 412. Take the Adams Road exit and go
south through the light to the parking lot. Boom there it is.

Restored Fire House
Tulsa / Sand Springs, OK

Located at 345 S 41st W Ave, Tulsa, OK, 74127, this vintage Fire Station #13 in Tulsa County is on Charles Page Blvd., heading west towards Sand Springs on the south side of the road is a site worth checking out. Only mere minutes west of downtown Tulsa you won't be far from the Outsiders house, Cain's Ballroom, Church Studio or the oddly placed Indian burial ground in the middle of a Sand Springs parking lot just a few miles further down this road. Definitely a day trip destination to see and perhaps take pictures of your classic car out front.

World's Tallest Gas Pump
Sapulpa, OK

On the north side of Route 66 heading west out of Sapulpa. Next door to the Route 66 Auto Museum.

Bronze Buffalo
Sapulpa, OK

On the north Side of Route 66 heading west into Sapulpa.

*********76*********

Bumblebee Transformer Stillwater, OK

One of two large Transformers located in Stillwater, OK. This over 20 ft. tall replica of Bumblebee is located at: G&M Body Shop in Stillwater. Located on the north side of Hwy 51 on the west side of Stillwater, next to El Vaquero Mexican restaurant and Motel 6, it is quite the site. Bumblebee is six miles down 6th street from the other location where Optimus Prime is located. It was originally built in Thailand and then brought to the USA and upgraded by body shop owner Mike McCubbin. It is one of five in the USA over 20 ft. tall.

*********77*********

Tam Bao Buddhist Temple & Statue – Tulsa, OK

Located at: 16933 E 21st St, Tulsa, OK, 74134. This ornate temple boasts a 50 ft. tall Buddhist deity statue, America's largest. Gates are open Friday – Sunday. For more information call 918-438-0714. A calm, authentic, impressive, location and spiritual experience. A must see!

Sam Kinison's Grave
Tulsa, OK

Memorial Park Cemetery located on southeast edge of the city. The cemetery entrance is on the southeast corner of S. Memorial Drive and E. 51st St. S. Sec. 28, Lot 92, Space 3

The Cave House
Tulsa, OK

The Cave House, a former chicken restaurant / speakeasy. Built into the side of the hill located at: 1623 Charles Page Blvd, Tulsa, OK, 74127. A very unique structure built in the 1920's. It is said to once have had tunnels through a passageway leading to a secret room that was a speakeasy at night. The house has a unique history of unusual tenants. Make sure and stop by for a tour and check it out.

**********80**********

Outsiders Movie House Tulsa, OK

The house from the Francis Ford Coppola 80's movie *The Outsiders*. Now a museum and gift shop. Located at: 731 N. St. Louis Tulsa, OK. Stop by for a tour of the museum and cool memorabilia. www.theoutsidershouse.com

Tulsa Air and Space Museum
Tulsa, OK

Located at: 3624 N 74th E Ave, Tulsa, OK, 74115, the Tulsa Air and Space Museum located on the northwest corner of the Tulsa International Airport property. It has about 19,000 sq. ft. of exhibits, activities, and vintage aircraft, also boasting a full-dome planetarium. Founded in 1998 the Tulsa Air and Space Museum is a must see. For more information call (918) 834-9900. www.tulsamuseum.org

VW Bug Spider Sculpture
Tulsa, OK

Located at Emtech Pest Control, 1241 North Sheridan Rd, Tulsa, OK, east side of Sheridan Rd at Newton St. which is North of I-244 and south of Pine St. This sculpture body is a VW bug lifted up in the air on metal legs. This cool looking "bug" is one of the 8 legged variety unlike many others across the country that only have 6 legs. It's worth the quick detour to check out if you are in the Tulsa area.

Muffler Man Cowboy Statue Wynnewood, OK

This particular "giant cowboy" was used in the movie Twister but was cut from the film. It was purchased by Steppin Out Western Wear, and in 2008 was moved to Wynnewood, OK. He was repaired and displayed until he was blown down in December 2011. Since then he has been repaired once again and is still standing at the site. Located at: 35646 Hwy 2, Wynnewood, OK, 73075, check this roadside giant out. A cousin to Tulsa's Buck Atom he's worth the drive.

Roadside Space Capsule Winganon, OK

An abandoned cement mixer on the side of the road that has been there for years and years painted to look like a vintage space capsule is a unique sight for sure. Located east of U.S. Route 75 on E 300 Road in Talala, OK. An interesting roadside stop for the day trip enthusiast.

**********85**********

National Cowboy Hall of Fame – OKC, OK

Founded 1955 in Oklahoma City. Located at: 1700 NE 63rd St, Oklahoma City, OK, 73111. The museum boasts more than 28,000 Western and American Indian art works and artifacts. The N.C.H.o.F. also has the world's most extensive collection of American rodeo photographs, barbed wire, saddlery, and early rodeo trophies. More information and hours of operation can be found online at www.nationalcowboymuseum.org.

**********86**********

Oklahoma Music Hall of Fame – Muskogee, OK

Located at: 401 S 3rd St Muskogee, OK, 74401, the Oklahoma Music Hall of Fame honors Oklahoma musicians that have significantly contributed to the local and national music scene. Artists such as Leon Russell, Garth Brooks and Roy Clark have been inducted. Worth the short drive to Muskogee to check out the museum and explore all of the amazing inducted musicians from Oklahoma.

Great Salt Plains State Park
Jet, OK

The Great Salt Plains State Park located in Alfalfa County, Oklahoma, is a 840-acre Oklahoma state park. The park is located 8 miles north of Jet, Oklahoma, on SH-38 and 12 miles east of Cherokee at 23280 S. Spillway Dr, Jet, OK, 73749. The landscape of the Salt Plains National Wildlife Refuge is comprised of salt leftover from an ocean that covered Oklahoma in prehistoric times.

Visitors can take their pick of activities such as riding on the bike trails. Equestrians can bring their own horses to ride trails. There are beautiful nature trails to enjoy while taking in the scenery. Fishing is available at the lake and is fun for the entire family. There are many varieties of fish such as catfish, sand bass, and hybrid stripers can be found in these salty, shallow waters. Canoeing and Kayaking is also allowed.

There is also a very unique crystal digging area which is open from April 1 to October 15 from sunrise to sunset. The crystals located just under the surface of the salt plains, form into an hourglass shape. Oklahoma is the only place known in the world where the hourglass-shaped selenite crystal can be found.

A day trip worth spending a few days there.

**************88**************

Price Tower
Bartlesville, OK

This unique tower was designed by famous architect Frank Lloyd Wright and built in 1956. 19 floors, and 42,000 sq. ft. It is 221 ft. tall and the only realized skyscraper by Wright. Located at: 510 South Dewey Ave. in Bartlesville, Oklahoma. The tower includes a hotel with unique mid century rooms, a lounge and arts center. A must see Oklahoma day trip destination.

**************89**************

Osteology Museum
OKC, OK

Located at: 10301 S Sunnylane Rd, Oklahoma City, OK, 73160, this museum celebrates all things vertebrate. The private museum is devoted to the study of bones and skeletons. The museum displays over 350 skeletons from many animal species all over the world. Plan your trip and call (405) 814-0006 for more information and hours of operation. No bones about it this is one you'll just be dying to check out.

Oklahoma Aquarium
Jenks, OK

The Oklahoma Aquarium is a 72,000-square-foot public aquarium built in 2002 in Jenks, OK, a suburb of Tulsa. The aquarium is home to the world's largest exhibit of bull sharks, as well as loggerhead sea turtles, zebra sharks and much more. Located at: 300 Aquarium Dr, Jenks, OK 74037 Call (918) 296-3474 for hours of operation and more information. Daily admission or yearly memberships available. Day trippin' to Jenks is a trip worth taking.

************91*********

Jim Thorpe Museum
OKC, OK

Located at 20 south Mickey Mantle Drive, Oklahoma City, Oklahoma, 73104. The Jim Thorpe Museum also includes The Oklahoma Sports Hall of Fame. Honoring Jim Thorpe and other Oklahoma athletes. This 10,000-square-foot, state-of-the-art museum offers free admission. A worthy Oklahoma day trip destination.

************92*********

Jim's Metal Art Museum
Gage, OK

Jim Powers, welder and artist, makes all kinds of unique sculptures displayed at this unusual museum. Unfortunately Jim Powers passed away in 2006 but his unique art created from cars and other junk he collected can still be seen in Gage, OK. Insects, buffalo, elephants, dinosaurs and more are still on display today. So, take a day trip adventure to Gage, OK, and check out Jim Powers unique art.

*********93*********

Tepee Church – Edmond, OK

Formerly Hopewell Baptist Church, this church has been abandoned for many years. Although recently it has had a new roof installed the tepee shaped building sits in disrepair. If you like unique and unusual architecture and structures you won't want to miss this one. Located at: NW 178 and N MacArthur Boulevard in Edmond, OK.

*********94*********

Gandini's Circus
Edmond, OK

Located in Edmond, Oklahoma, up the street from the local Sonic Drive-In at North Kelly Avenue between Swan Lake Road and Pruett Drive is Gandini's Circus. The exact reason it is named that is a mystery but the decaying remains still stand slowly decaying. Though located on private property you can still glimpse from the road these ghostly reminders of times past. Legend says Gandini's began in the early 1900's and went under during the Great Depression. A neat day trip destination of mystery if you are out near Edmond, Oklahoma.

More information at:
www.atlasobscura.com/places/gandinis-circus

Forgotten Wheels Museum
Davis, OK

Located at: 1775 US-77, Davis, OK, 73030, this museum has an intriguing collection of cars, wheels and antique sewing machines. Owned by Tom and Sandra Webb their unusual collections are worth the drive. There is an antique shop and you can even try out a vintage pedal sewing machine if you feel like being adventurous. Tom's teal '56 Chevy half-ton pickup that Grandpa Webb bought new is worth the trip by itself.

Harwelden Mansion
Tulsa, OK

Harwelden is a historical building and a Collegiate Gothic-English Tudor-style mansion in Tulsa, Oklahoma. Located at: 2210 S Main St, Tulsa, OK, on four acres. It was built in 1923 by a businessman and philanthropist, Earl P. Harwell. The mansion served as the headquarters for the Arts Council of Tulsa from 1969 to 2012. Currently the Historic Harwelden Mansion serves as a Corporate, Community, Wedding, Art, and Culture Venue and Event Center.

For booking information go check out their website at: https://harweldenmansion.com/ or call (918) 960-0714

Every other Thursday, the public can enjoy tours of the mansion, grounds and carriage house. The walking tours end with a proper cup of English tea and cookies. Guests learn about the Mansion's history, the Harwell family, architecture, renovations and the Mansion's programming.

Individual rooms or entire floors can be rented in the 15,000 sq. ft. mansion. Six luxury bedroom suites are available to reserve for overnight guests. The mansion is ideal for weddings, corporate retreats, nonprofit fundraisers, art exhibits or musical performances to name a few. Outdoor tented events work out beautifully surrounded by native gardens and stunning landscape and riverfront views. Individuals and groups will enjoy the unique experience the mansion brings.

*********97*********

Mayo Hotel – Tulsa, OK

Located downtown at: 115 W 5th St, Tulsa, OK, 74103, the Mayo is a historic Art Deco hotel opened in 1925 and is a short five to ten minute walk from the many other rich experiences downtown Tulsa has to offer. Check out their website at: themayohotel.com or call (918) 582-6296 truly an experience you won't soon forget.

Jim Thorpe Home and Park
Yale, OK

Located at 706 East Boston Avenue Yale, Oklahoma, 74085, is a little house Jim Thorpe bought and resided in from 1917 until 1923. The park is on the east end of Yale just off of highway 51. This day trip to Yale, Oklahoma, is a great way to spend the day learning about Jim Thorpe and enjoying a quiet country town and all it has to offer.

Tydol Oil Refinery
Drumright, OK

The Tidewater Oil Company (Tydol) was a major petroleum refining and marketing company for more than 80 years, known for its Flying A-brand products and gas stations.

A large refinery was built in Drumright which was the center of the Tydol community. It was the needs of this growing community that spawned the building of the historic Tidal School, now the Tidewater Winery. This 8,000 sq. ft. building was built by John D. Rockefeller in the 1920's during Drumright's oil boom, later acquired by J.

Paul Getty, and is listed on the national register of historic places.

When the refinery closed, many families from this community moved. The remains of the refinery are a few buildings, foundations and furnaces and the Getty office building. The Tydol community virtually disappeared with the exception of the school. In the 1960's the remaining community was called Tydol Camp. The current owner of Tidewater Winery spent her teenage years living in the "Camp" in a company house owned by Getty Oil. The now abandoned Getty Oil Company office remains at the top of the hill and some local families still live in what was called Tydol Camp.

A wonderfully historic site to visit, just a short drive off Route 66 on Highway 16 south of Drumright.

********100********

Eastern State Hospital
Vinita, OK

Located at: 442104 E 250 Rd, Vinita, OK, 74301, this abandoned hospital was finished in 1912 on a 160 acre tract. While other buildings occupy the property this abandoned hospital with its creepy history is a site worth driving by and seeing if you are up that way.

More info at: abandonedok.com/eastern-state-hospital/

******Bonus*******

"The Rock Crusher"
Sand Springs, OK

On the south side of the road just before Hwy 51 junctions with Hwy 97 in Sand Springs, south of the Arkansas River bridge. This structure is referred to as "The Rock Crusher" by many locals. In recent years the city of Sand Springs has undergone many changes including the addition of some murals on the face of this unique structure. Definitely a sight to see.

*******Bonus*******

Bob Wills Grave – Tulsa, OK

Located in Memorial Park Cemetery at 51st and Memorial in Tulsa, Oklahoma. Section 15, Lot 560, Space 2

The late great Bob Wills and his Texas Playboys are very much a part of Tulsa's music history and the history of Cain's Ballroom. While visiting Tulsa stop by Memorial Park Cemetery and pay your respects to Bob and other Oklahoma legends like Leon Russell, Sam Kinison and Roy Clark all in close proximity to one another.

Roy Clark Grave – Tulsa, OK

Located in Memorial Park Cemetery at 51st and Memorial in Tulsa, Oklahoma. Section 15A, Estate 15, Space 1

Roy Clark is yet another Tulsa Music legend. Whether you liked Roy's country music or laughed at Roy on Hee-Haw you should stop by and pay your respects to this country music legend. Just around the corner from Leon Russell, Bob Wills and Sam Kinison.

If you get lost in this large cemetery the nice ladies in the main office on the corner will be glad to give you directions.

*******Themes*******

Legends:

7. Leon Russell Monument (Memorial Park Tulsa)

26. Star Walk of Fame (Downtown Tulsa)

34. Mount Olive Cemetery (Phil Seymour) (Hugo, OK)

53. Mickey Mantle Statue #1 (Commerce, OK)

54. Tom Mix Museum (Dewey, OK)

59. Woody Guthrie Statue (Okemah, OK)

60. Woody Guthrie Home Site (Okemah, OK)

63. Mickey Mantle Statue #2 (OKC, OK)

64. Vince Gill Statue (OKC, OK)

78. Grave of Sam Kinison (Memorial Cemetery Tulsa)

98. Jim Thorpe Home & Park (Yale, OK)

Bonus 2: Bob Wills Grave (Memorial Cemetery Tulsa)

Bonus 3: Roy Clark Grave (Memorial Cemetery Tulsa)

*******Themes*******

Music Sites:

1. Church Studio and Museum (Tulsa)

5. Cain's Ballroom (Downtown Tulsa)

7. Leon Russell Monument (Memorial Park Tulsa)

10. Woody Guthrie Center (Downtown Tulsa)

11. OK Jazz Hall of Fame (Downtown Tulsa)

20. Leon Russell Murals (Near Downtown Tulsa)

26. Star Walk of Fame (Downtown Tulsa)

27. OKPOP Museum (Downtown Tulsa)

34. Mount Olive Cemetery (Phil Seymour) (Hugo, OK)

59. Woody Guthrie Statue (Okemah, OK)

60. Woody Guthrie Home Site (Okemah, OK)

62. Flaming Lips Alley (OKC, OK)

64. Vince Gill Statue (OKC, OK)

86. OK Music Hall of Fame (Muskogee, OK)

Bonus 2: Bob Wills Grave (Memorial Cemetery Tulsa)

Bonus 3: Roy Clark Grave (Memorial Cemetery Tulsa)

*******Themes*******

Large Statues & Sculptures:

2. Center of the Universe (Downtown Tulsa)

3. Golden Driller (Midtown Tulsa)

4. Blue Whale (Catoosa, OK)

6. Giant Indian Chief (Big Cabin, OK)

8. Praying Hands (ORU Campus - Tulsa, OK)

17. Buck Atom's (Near Downtown Tulsa)

25. Optimus Prime Statue (Stillwater, OK)

28. World's Tallest Totem Pole (Foyil, OK)

39. Pop's Pop Bottle Sculpture

51. Life Size Metal Dinosaur

52. Tin Woodsman

53. Mickey Mantle Statue #1 (Commerce, OK)

55. World's Largest Peanut

56. VW Bug Spider #1

59. Woody Guthrie Statue (Okemah, OK)

63. Mickey Mantle Statue #2 (OKC, OK)

64. Vince Gill Statue (OKC, OK)

67. Giant Pioneer Woman & Museum

68. Standing Bear

69. Howdy Tire Man

70. Dinosaur and Space Rocket

74. World's Tallest Gas Pump (Sapulpa, OK)

75. Bronze Buffalo Statue (Sapulpa, OK)

77. Tam Bao Buddhist Temple & Statue (Tulsa, OK)

82. VW Bug Spider #2

83. Muffler Man Cowboy Statue

84. Space Capsule Sculpture

******Itineraries******

(Make your own trip)

1.

2.

3.

4.

5.

6.

7.

8.

9.

10.

11.

12.

13.

14.

15.

16.

17.

About the author: Knoel C. Honn

A native of Tulsa, Oklahoma, and a graduate of Rogers State University in Claremore, Oklahoma. Knoel has pursued different aspects of music and writing for many years. As a photographer, artist, musician, poet, and author Knoel enjoys traveling his home state and the country. After many of his day trips around Oklahoma Knoel decided to write this book on several of his favorite spots.

Knoel has also recently published the book *Recalling The Call* about the 80's rock band The Call. It is an exciting and thoughtful look into one of the most underrated bands in rock 'n roll history.

For more information check out *Recalling The Call* or *The Call 40* on Facebook or www.ExoticOkie.com to buy his books.